BENJAMIN *Franklin*

SPIRIT
of America®

BENJAMIN *Franklin*

PRINTER, SCIENTIST, AUTHOR, AND DIPLOMAT

By Ann Heinrichs

Content Adviser: James Srodes, author of Franklin: The Essential Founding Father

The
**Child's
World**

The Child's World®
Chanhassen, Minnesota

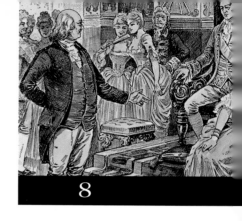

8

BENJAMIN *Franklin*

Published in the United States of America by The Child's World®
PO Box 326 • Chanhassen, MN 55317-0326 • 800-599-READ • www.childsworld.com

Acknowledgments
The Child's World®: Mary Berendes, Publishing Director

Editorial Directions, Inc.: E. Russell Primm, Editorial Director; Pam Rosenberg, Line Editor; Katie Marsico, Assistant Editor; Matthew Messbarger, Editorial Assistant; Susan Hindman, Copy Editor; Susan Ashley, Proofreader; Julie Zaveloff, Chris Simms, and Peter Garnham, Fact Checkers; Tim Griffin/IndexServ, Indexer; Dawn Friedman, Photo Researcher; Linda S. Koutris, Photo Selector

The Design Lab: Kathleen Petelinsek, Art Direction; Kari Thornborough, Page Production

Photo
Cover and page 2: The Corcoran Gallery of Art/Corbis; National Portrait Gallery, Smithsonian Institution/Art Resource, NY: 27; The Corcoran Gallery of Art/Corbis: 2; Bettmann/Corbis: 6, 16; Kelly Harriger/Corbis: 10; Corbis: 18; Joseph Sohm, ChromoSohm, Inc./Corbis: 28; Hulton|Archive/ Getty Images: 14, 19, 23, 24; Kean Collection/Getty Images: 12; The Granger Collection, New York: 7, 13, 26; Library of Congress: 20; North Wind Picture Archives: 8, 11, 22.

Registration
The Child's World®, Spirit of America®, and their associated logos are the sole property and registered trademarks of The Child's World®.

Library of Congress Cataloging-in-Publication Data
Heinrichs, Ann.
   Benjamin Franklin : printer, scientist, author, and diplomat / by Ann Heinrichs.
      v. cm. — (Our people)
   Includes index.
   Contents: A man for all people—Changing minds, changing lives—The public servant—Building a new nation.
   ISBN 1-59296-173-8 (lib. bdg. : alk. paper)
   1. Franklin, Benjamin, 1706–1790—Juvenile literature. 2. Statesmen—United States—Biography—Juvenile literature. 3. Scientists—United States—Biography—Juvenile literature. 4. Inventors—United States—Biography—Juvenile literature. 5. Printers—United States—Biography—Juvenile literature. [1. Franklin, Benjamin, 1706–1790. 2. Statesmen. 3. Scientists. 4. Inventors. 5. Printers.] I. Title. II. Series.
   E302.6.F8 H45 2004
   973.3'092—dc22   2003018119

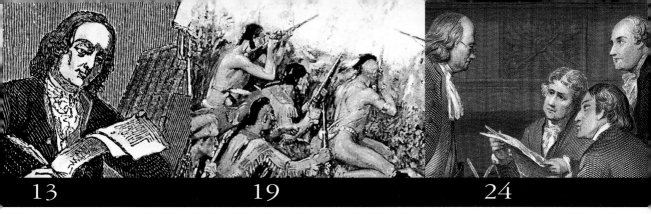

13   19   24

Contents

Chapter ONE   *A Man for All People*   6

Chapter TWO   *Changing Minds,*   12
                   Changing Lives

Chapter THREE   *The Public Servant*   18

Chapter FOUR   *Building a New Nation*   24

                   Time Line   29

                   Glossary Terms   30

                   For Further Information   31

                   Index   32

A Man for All People

THAT AFTERNOON IN JUNE 1752 WAS DARK WITH frightening storm clouds. Benjamin Franklin stood sheltered in the doorway of an empty barn. He held tight to a kite string, his eyes trained on the kite flap-

Before Franklin's legendary kite experiment, many people thought that electricity was made up of two opposing forces. Franklin proved that electricity consisted of a "common element" which he gave the name "electric fire."

ping higher toward the dark sky. Just inches from his hand, a key dangled from the string. On the floor was a bottle-shaped storage battery that he had built.

As drops of rain began to fall and then pour from the sky, Franklin saw fibers of the string begin to rise and stand stiffly. An electrical charge coursed down the string toward the key. Carefully, Franklin moved his knuckle toward the key and was rewarded with a crackling spark. Excitedly, he pulled the string and key close to the storage battery and filled it with the electrical charge so he could carry it home to his laboratory.

This dangerous experiment could have killed Franklin. Yet he was willing to risk his life to prove his **theory** that lightning was simply a current of electricity. The key had captured the storm's electrical energy. People could save their homes from fires caused by lightning, Franklin said, if they attached an iron spike to the roof. Like the key, this lightning rod would draw off the electricity and keep the building safe. Electricity also could be harnessed for use in other ways, he believed. It could be used to cook foods, to heat rooms, and to perform many other chores.

The lightning rod was just one of Benjamin Franklin's many inventions. He

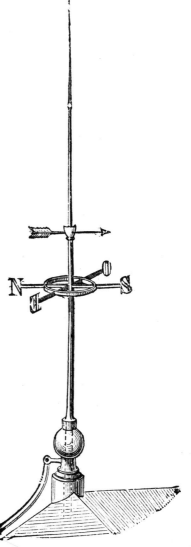

Franklin rigged his lightning rod to draw lighting down into his house. The rod was connected to two bells, one of which was connected to a ground wire. Every time there was an electrical storm, bells would ring and ding and sparks would light up his house.

The French court loved Benjamin Franklin's witty ways and love of a good time. France sided with the Americans largely because of Franklin's trustworthiness and his good humor.

never took out a patent on any of his inventions. Instead, he wanted everyone to be free to experiment with his inventions and improve them.

Franklin was dedicated to making everyday life better for the average citizen. He was much more than an inventor, though. Benjamin Franklin was a brilliant man with many talents. He is considered one of the greatest Americans in history.

Franklin is one of America's Founding Fathers. His **outspoken** views were known throughout the American colonies. As a **diplomat,** he tried to keep peace between Great Britain and the colonies. In spite of his efforts, the Revolutionary War (1775–1783) broke out. Yet, because Franklin was able to persuade France to join the war on the American side, the colonies gained their freedom. Franklin also

8

played an important role in starting the government of the new country. He helped create both the Declaration of Independence and the U.S. Constitution.

Benjamin Franklin was born on January 17, 1706, in Boston, Massachusetts. His parents were Josiah and Abiah Folger Franklin. Benjamin was the 15th of their 17 children. Josiah made soap and candles in his shop on Boston's Milk Street. This was not such an odd combination of products. Both soap and candles were made from tallow, or animal fat.

Benjamin went to work in his father's shop at the age of 10. He filled the candle-dipping molds, trimmed the wicks, and ran errands. "I disliked the trade, and had a strong inclination for the sea," Franklin wrote, "but my father declared against it."

At 12, Benjamin became an **apprentice** in the printing shop that belonged to his brother James. There he learned the printer's trade, which he would follow later in life. Benjamin had only two years of schooling. But don't think for a minute that his education stopped! On his own, he devoured books by many great writers. They ranged from the ancient Greek writer Plutarch to the British minister John Bunyan.

Benjamin sometimes wrote poems that were printed in James's shop. One told the adventures of the pirate Blackbeard. Benjamin's father, however, discouraged the young poet. "Verse-makers were generally beggars," he warned. After that, Benjamin

Interesting Fact

▶ When he was a boy, Franklin invented two devices to help him swim. One was a set of oval paddles worn on the hands and feet. Another was a kite to drag him through the water as he floated on his back. Later, he wrote a how-to manual on swimming. After his death, Franklin was inducted into the International Swimming Hall of Fame.

turned his efforts to **prose.** He read the British journal *The Spectator* and tried to imitate its style.

Benjamin hated working for his bossy brother. Later in life, he said his love for independence was born during that time. The two brothers often quarreled. Benjamin confessed that "perhaps I was too saucy and provoking." Nevertheless, "I took upon me to assert my freedom."

In 1723, at age 17, Benjamin ran off to Philadelphia, Pennsylvania. This would be his home for the rest of his life.

Independence Hall (right) in Philadelphia, Pennsylvania was the site of many important events leading to the birth of the United States. Construction of the building began in 1732, nine years after Franklin chose Philadelphia as his new home.

BENJAMIN'S BROTHER JAMES PUBLISHED A NEWSPAPER CALLED THE *New-England Courant.* Young Benjamin secretly sent letters to the paper, signing them with the made-up name Silence Dogood.

Mrs. Dogood was the witty widow of a country minister. She poked fun at New England's wealthy, upper-class people for their ignorance and foolishness. Here are some of her comments.

On a dishonest government official: His first act is "to betray the best Men in his Country into an Opinion of his Goodness." The people "take him for a Saint . . . and ruin their Country for God's sake."

On a minister who becomes a lawyer: He "is able to cheat a whole Country with his Religion, and then destroy them under Colour of Law."

On someone who drinks too much: "He retain'd only the Shape of a Man, and acted the Part of a Beast."

On ladies' hoopskirts: "These monstrous topsy-turvy Mortar-Pieces, are neither fit for the Church, the Hall, or the Kitchen." They "look more like Engines of War for bombarding the Town, than Ornaments of the Fair Sex."

Chapter TWO

Changing Minds, Changing Lives

"I WAS DIRTY FROM MY JOURNEY, MY POCKETS WERE stuff'd out with shirts and stockings, and I knew no soul nor where to look for lodging."

This is how Franklin described his arrival in Philadelphia. Tired and hungry, he made his way

In Franklin's retelling of the story of his arrival in Philadelphia, he said that he happened to pass by the house of his future wife Deborah Read. She thought he looked odd and never imagined that she would marry him seven years later.

to a bakery. He asked for three pennies' worth of bread and got "three great puffy rolls." Then, "having no room in my pockets, walk'd off with a roll under each arm, and eating the other."

Franklin soon found work with a printer. By 1728, he was able to open his own print shop. Franklin used his printing press to change people's lives for the better. One way he did this was to share his wisdom. He invented a character named Poor Richard.

Poor Richard was full of wise and witty sayings. Each one was a lesson in **thrift,** hard work, and common sense. Franklin published these

Interesting Fact

▸ In 1734, Franklin acknowledged his gratitude to his "Courteous Readers" for purchasing so many of his almanacs. Their generosity, he said allowed his wife to buy a cooking pot of her own, a pair of shoes, two new shifts, and a warm petticoat. He went on to say that these things made her much happier which, in turn, allowed him to sleep better.

BENJAMIN FRANKLIN BEGAN PUBLISHING *POOR RICHARD'S ALMANACK* IN 1733. A new **almanac** came out every year for 26 years. It contained weather forecasts, sunrise and sunset times, movements of the moon and planets, and much more. But the almanac is best known for Poor Richard's wise sayings.

Poor Richard gave advice on how to get ahead in the world. He opposed any sort of foolishness. He urged hard work and discouraged wasting time and money. Here are some of Poor Richard's sayings. What do you think each one means?

▸ God helps them that help themselves.
▸ An ounce of prevention is worth a pound of cure.
▸ Early to bed and early to rise makes a man healthy, wealthy, and wise.
▸ One today is worth two tomorrows.
▸ The doors of wisdom are never shut.
▸ A lie stands on one leg, the truth on two.
▸ Well done is better than well said.
▸ A good example is the best sermon.
▸ Three may keep a secret, if two of them are dead.
▸ Little strokes fell great oaks.
▸ Whatever is begun in anger ends in shame.

152   *A New Guide*

A Bird in the Hand is worth two in the Bush.

FABLE XII. *Of the Fisherman and the Fish.*

A Fisherman having cast his Line into the Water, presently after drew up a Fish.

The little Captive entreated the Fisherman that he would spare her (she being but small) till she was grown larger; then she would suffer herself to be taken by him again.

No, no, replies the Fisherman, I am not to be so served: If I let you go, I must never expect to see you any more; neither should I have caught you now, if you had known there was a Hook within the Bait: And I was always of that Temper, that whatever I could catch, I had rather take it away than leave it behind me.

The Interpretation.

Never let go a Certainty for an Uncertainty.

sayings in *Poor Richard's Almanack*. Many popular sayings today are the words of Franklin, speaking as Poor Richard.

Franklin also published a newspaper called *The Pennsylvania Gazette*. The *Gazette* gave him a chance to put his ideas about news into action. Franklin wanted the news to come alive for his readers. He printed illustrations and maps with his news stories. He even included political cartoons. He believed that even people who had trouble reading could understand the news.

In 1730, Franklin married Deborah Read. They later had a son, Francis, who died at age four, and a daughter, Sarah. The couple also raised Franklin's son William, whose mother is unknown. The Franklins had a print shop, a general store, and a bookstore. Deborah helped run the shops while raising the children.

Franklin started a club called the Junto, or Leather Apron Club. Its members discussed scientific, political, and moral issues of the day. Franklin used the Junto to introduce many of his ideas for a better society. They included a city police force and a city fire department.

Franklin sold his printing business in 1748. Then he devoted himself to politics and science. Benjamin had been curious about science since childhood. He wanted to know how things worked—and how they could work better. This

In 1731, Franklin organized the Library Company of Philadelphia. It was the first lending library in the colonies. Franklin established Philadelphia's Union Fire Company in 1736. It was America's first fire department. He also founded America's first fire insurance company. Franklin founded the Academy of Philadelphia in 1751. It grew to become the University of Pennsylvania.

was just another way to make everyday life easier for common people.

In the 1700s, electricity was a fad, good for tricks at parties. For Franklin, however, electricity was a science mystery to explore. His best-known electrical experiment was his famous kite stunt. He used his discovery about lightning to invent the lightning rod.

Like many people of his time, Franklin had poor eyesight. Whenever he wanted to read, he

Benjamin Franklin made life easier for many people when he invented bifocals.

16

had to take off his regular glasses and put on reading glasses. This annoyed him constantly. Finally, he took both pairs of glasses and cut the lenses in half. He arranged the halves so that the reading lenses were on the bottom. Now we call these glasses bifocals.

Another invention was the Franklin stove. It was an iron chest with a fire blazing inside. The stove was much safer than an open fireplace. Sparks couldn't pop out and set accidental fires. The stove gave off much more heat than a fireplace, too.

Franklin served as postmaster of Philadelphia from 1737 to 1753. As he rode along his delivery route, he began to wonder how far he traveled every day. He invented a device that attached to his carriage wheels and counted the miles they covered as they turned. This was the first odometer. These mileage-counting devices are standard equipment in every vehicle today.

Franklin's ideas and inventions had a big impact on colonial life. Many of his ideas—such as fire insurance and lending libraries—are still part of life today. Franklin's greatest achievements, however, were yet to come. He was elected to the Pennsylvania Assembly, or lawmaking body, in 1750. Then he began his career in public service.

Chapter THREE

The Public Servant

Benjamin Franklin's illustration, "Join, or Die," is considered to be the first political cartoon in America. The "Join, or Die" cartoon was published in almost every newspaper on the continent.

JOIN, OR DIE. THAT WAS THE TITLE OF BENJAMIN Franklin's first political cartoon. It appeared in *The Pennsylvania Gazette* in 1754. It pictured a snake cut into several sections, each labeled with a colony's initials. The message was clear: The colonies must unite, or the whole organism would die.

For Franklin, this cartoon was no joke. He had just met with representatives of seven colonies in Albany, New York. There he presented his Plan of Union. It was a plan for all 13 colonies to elect delegates to a colonial assembly led by a royal governor. This assembly would take care of matters that affected all of the colonies. One big concern in-

volved France and Great Britain, which were at war in Europe. Their war had now spilled over into North America. These conflicts were called the French and Indian War (1754–1763). The colonial assembly would help the colonies unite to deal with the problems brought about by the war being fought on their land.

The Albany Congress approved Franklin's Plan of Union. The next step was for all 13 colonies to ratify it. That was when Franklin rushed back to Philadelphia and published his cartoon. He also wrote articles in the *Gazette*. However, the colonies did not approve the plan.

The French and Indian War between the British and the French was a threat to the colonists in America. Franklin helped get money for forts to be built in Pennsylvania. Franklin himself served as Colonel Commander of the Philadelphia armed forces during the French and Indian War.

Benjamin Franklin presents the concerns of the American colonists to the British Lords at Whitehall Chapel in London in 1774.

But Franklin knew that, sooner or later, they would have to join together—or die.

Meanwhile, the Pennsylvania Colony was in a bit of trouble. The French and Indian War was costing the colony a lot of money. William Penn had founded the colony in 1681. Penn belonged to the Quaker religion, which was opposed to war. Now Penn's descendants refused to pay taxes on their land because they were against the war. But the colony badly needed the tax money.

In 1757, the Pennsylvania Assembly sent Franklin to London, England. He was to ask the king for the right to tax the Penns' land. He succeeded, but his work was far from over. For the next several years, Franklin represented the American colonies in Great Britain.

Franklin loved living in London. He made many new friends there and enjoyed discussing new ideas with them. He felt friendly and loyal toward England and was glad to help the colonies work out their problems. He was sure things could be worked out by discussion. However, Franklin would begin to doubt this.

In 1765, the British Parliament, or lawmaking body, passed the Stamp Act to help pay the high cost of the French and Indian War. Under this law, all legal documents and printed material such as newspapers and playing cards had to have special stamps attached to them. The colonists would have to buy the stamps. Many colonists were strongly opposed to this new tax. Soon the cry arose: "No taxation without representation!" Delegates from nine colonies met and declared the Stamp Act illegal.

In 1766, Franklin appeared before the Parliament's House of Commons. He answered questions about taxation and the bad effects it had on the colonies. One after another, the members hurled questions at him. Franklin kept his cool. He answered a total of 174 questions, always stressing that the colonists needed to have a voice in their own government. A month later, Parliament repealed the Stamp Act.

The colonists' troubles were far from over. In 1773, Parliament passed the Tea Act. It charged duties, or import taxes, on tea shipped to the colonies.

▶ Franklin's face appears on the U.S. $100 bill.

THE TEA ACT WAS UNFAIR TO THE COLONISTS IN MANY WAYS. IT MADE THE British East India Company the only legal seller of tea in the colonies. The act also enabled the company to sell tea cheaper than anyone else. In addition, the colonists had to pay taxes on the tea. Throughout the colonies, people protested by refusing to buy British tea. The biggest protest took place in Boston.

On the night of December 16, 1773, about 60 Bostonians gathered at the harbor. They were crudely disguised as Mohawk Indians, wearing blankets over their shoulders and feathers on their heads. Very quietly, they boarded three British ships—the *Dartmouth, Eleanor,* and *Beaver.* Then they broke open 342 chests of tea and dumped them into the sea.

Britain punished the colonists with the **Intolerable** Acts. One of these laws closed Boston's port to sea trade.

In protest, colonists raided three ships in Boston Harbor. Dressed as Native Americans, they dumped the ships' cargo of tea into the harbor. This was called the Boston Tea Party.

Franklin still hoped the colonies could stay on good terms with Britain. He even offered to pay for the tea if Britain would repeal the Tea Act. But it was no use. His appeals fell on deaf ears.

In 1774, Parliament cracked down and passed even harsher laws. Colonists called them the Intolerable Acts. Finally, the colonists united to oppose British rule. They formed the First Continental Congress. Sadly, Franklin realized that he could do no more. He boarded a ship for home on March 21, 1775. During his six weeks at sea, the Revolutionary War broke out in the colonies.

Interesting Fact

▶ Benjamin Franklin's son, William, was the royal governor of the New Jersey Colony. Franklin was deeply disappointed that William supported Great Britain instead of the colonists. Near the end of his life, Franklin wrote to his son, "Nothing has ever hurt me with such keen sensations, as to find myself deserted in my old age by my only son; and . . . to find him taking up arms against me in a cause wherein my good fame, fortune and life were all at stake."

On September 5, 1774, all the colonies except Georgia sent their representatives to what we now refer to as the First Continental Congress. The meeting was held in secret so that the British would not know that the colonies were uniting.

23

Chapter FOUR

Building a New Nation

FRANKLIN'S SHIP SAILED INTO PHILADELPHIA HARBOR on May 5, 1775. He barely had a moment to catch his breath. The very next day, Philadelphians chose him as a delegate to the Second Continental Congress.

Thomas Jefferson (center) was put in charge of writing the first draft of the Declaration of Independence. Franklin was not in good health, so instead of writing the Declaration of Independence, he reviewed it and made slight changes.

Fighting between British troops and colonists was growing worse. For the Continental Congress, the only choice seemed to be to break away from Great Britain. Franklin was one of five men chosen to turn this bold idea into a document. The result was the Declaration of Independence. Along with 55 other delegates, Franklin signed the declaration on July 4, 1776. At age 70, he was the oldest person to sign it.

Franklin was an old man by now, but he was about to take on the most important job of his life. The war was not going well for the colonists. The British army was more experienced and better equipped than the Continental army. Without more troops, they might lose their chances for freedom. In late 1776, Congress sent Franklin to Paris, France. His job was to persuade the French to become allies of the United States against Great Britain.

France was in no hurry to go to war with Great Britain, but Franklin patiently stuck to his mission. In October 1777, the tides turned. The colonial army scored a great victory over the British at Saratoga, New York. The French were so impressed that they agreed to join the war on the colonists' side. Franklin helped draw up the Treaty of **Alliance,** and it was signed on February 6, 1778. With France's help, the Americans won the Revolutionary War. In 1783, Franklin helped draw up the Treaty of Paris, which officially ended the war.

Interesting Fact

▸ John Hancock of Massachusetts spoke to those gathered to sign the Declaration of Independence. He said that the delegates must be unified in their decision. Franklin replied, "We must indeed all hang together, or, most assuredly, we shall all hang separately."

At last, in 1785, Franklin returned to Philadelphia. By this time, he was in great pain from a stone in his bladder. Though he led a quiet life, he still took part in shaping his new nation. The state of Pennsylvania appointed him president of its executive council. That post was much like the job of governor today.

The states held a Constitutional Convention in 1787. Its members drew up the U.S. Constitution—a basic set of rules and principles upon which the nation would stand. Pennsylvania sent Franklin as a delegate to the convention. Now 81, he was once again the oldest member there. The beloved old man had many illnesses by now. He was often carried to the meetings in a **sedan chair.**

George Washington (far right) presides over the Constitutional Convention. All of the delegates at the convention, had very different ideas about how the country should be run. Franklin felt strongly that the executive branch had too much power placed in one person and that some kind of committee would be the better option.

Large and small states argued bitterly over how they could have an equal voice in the new U.S. Congress. Franklin came up with a solution. He suggested a Congress with two houses—a Senate and a House of Representatives. Members of the House of Representatives would be elected according to a state's population. The Senate would have two members from each state, regardless of size. As we know, this plan was adopted.

Franklin retired from public life and, by 1789, was confined to his bed. But he did not stop working for causes he believed in. He became the first president of the Pennsylvania Antislavery Society. It was the nation's first society dedicated to ending slavery.

Franklin now suffered from emphysema, a lung disease that makes it difficult to breathe. On April 17, 1790, he died at the age of 84. Twenty thousand people attended his funeral in Philadelphia. Among them were politicians, philosophers, and ordinary workers in the printing trade.

Benjamin Franklin arrived in Philadelphia as a penniless runaway. Through his inventions, wisdom, and skill, he changed the lives of countless

Toward the end of his life, Benjamin Franklin focused on the advancement of many liberal causes such as the abolition of slavery and granting the right to vote to as many people as possible.

people. He helped build a nation, and he brought many countries together in peace. After Franklin's death, Honoré-Gabriel Riqueti, Count of Mirabeau, a member of the French National Assembly, spoke of him. Franklin "was able to restrain alike thunderbolts and tyrants," he said.

He was "one of the greatest men who have ever been engaged in the service of philosophy and liberty."

Benjamin Franklin is buried in Christ Church burial ground, Philadelphia, next to his wife, Deborah, and his son Francis.

1706   Benjamin Franklin is born in Boston, Massachusetts, on January 17.

1718   Franklin begins working as a printer's apprentice for his brother James.

1723   Franklin leaves home and moves to Philadelphia, Pennsylvania.

1728   Franklin opens his own printing shop in Philadelphia.

1729–1766   *The Pennsylvania Gazette* is published by Franklin.

1730   Franklin marries Deborah Read.

1731   Franklin organizes the Library Company of Philadelphia.

1733–1758   *Poor Richard's Almanack* is published every year during this period.

1751   Franklin founds the Academy of Philadelphia. In time, it grows to become the University of Pennsylvania.

1752   Franklin performs his famous kite experiment to demonstrate that lightning is a form of electricity.

1754   Franklin presents his Plan of Union to colonial representatives in Albany, New York.

1766   Franklin appears before the British Parliament to argue against the Stamp Act and "taxation without representation."

1776   The Declaration of Independence is signed by Franklin and 55 other delegates.

1778   Franklin persuades France to become an ally of the American colonies against the British in the Revolutionary War.

1783   Franklin helps draw up the Treaty of Paris, which formally ends the Revolutionary War.

1787   Franklin is a delegate to the Constitutional Convention.

1789   Franklin becomes the first president of the Pennsylvania Antislavery Society.

1790   Franklin dies in Philadelphia on April 17. He is 84 years old.

alliance (uh-LYE-uhnss)
An alliance is an agreement between two countries to work together. Franklin helped draw up a treaty of alliance with France.

almanac (AWL-muh-nak)
An almanac is a yearly booklet with weather, astronomy, and other information. (It was spelled "almanack" in Franklin's day.) Franklin's *Poor Richard's Almanack* was a yearly booklet that included wise and witty sayings.

apprentice (uh-PREN-tiss)
An apprentice is a young worker who is learning a trade. Franklin began his printing career as an apprentice in his brother's printing shop.

diplomat (DIP-luh-mat)
A diplomat is an official who represents his or her country in another country. Franklin represented the colonies as a diplomat in England and France.

intolerable (in-TOL-ur-uh-buhl)
Something that is intolerable is harsh and unbearable. In 1774, Britain passed several harsh laws that the colonists called the Intolerable Acts.

outspoken (out-SPOH-kuhn)
Someone who is outspoken expresses his or her opinions in a clear and strong manner. Benjamin Franklin's outspoken views were well known throughout the colonies.

prose (PROZE)
Prose is writing that is not poetry. As a young man, Franklin wrote poetry but later changed to writing prose.

sedan chair (si-DAN CHAIR)
A sedan chair is a portable chair that is enclosed and mounted on horizontal poles. Benjamin Franklin was often carried to meetings in a sedan chair.

theory (THEE-ur-ee)
A theory is an idea that has not yet been proved scientifically. In his famous kite experiment, Franklin proved his theory that lightning is a form of electricity.

thrift (THRIFT)
Thrift is the habit of saving money and spending very carefully. In *Poor Richard's Almanack,* Franklin encouraged people to practice thrift.

For Further INFORMATION

Web Sites

Visit our home page for lots of links about Benjamin Franklin:
http://www.childsworld.com/links.html

Note to Parents, Teachers, and Librarians:
We routinely verify our Web links to make sure they're safe,
active sites—so encourage your readers to check them out!

Books

Giblin, James Cross, and Michael Dooling (illustrator). *The Amazing Life of Benjamin Franklin.* New York: Scholastic Press, 2000.

Glass, Maya. *Benjamin Franklin: Early American Genius.* New York: Rosen Publishing Group, 2003.

Sherrow, Victoria. *Benjamin Franklin.* Minneapolis: Lerner Publications, 2002.

Places to Visit or Contact

**Benjamin Franklin National Memorial
and Franklin Institute Science Museum**
To see many of Franklin's possessions and inventions
222 North 20th Street
Philadelphia, PA 19103
215/448-1200

Franklin Court
*To see many buildings associated with Franklin,
including a see-through model of his home*
316–322 Market Street (between 3rd and 4th Streets)
Philadelphia, PA 19106
215/597-8974

Index

Academy of Philadelphia, 15
armonica, 17

bifocals, 17
Boston, Massachusetts, 8, 9
Boston Tea Party, 22, *22,* 23
British East India Company, 22

colonies, 8, 15, 18, 19, 20, 21, 22, 23
Constitution of the United States, 9, 26, 27
Constitutional Convention, 26, *26*
currency, 21

Declaration of Independence, 9, *24,* 25, 27

electricity, 7, 16
emphysema, 27

First Continental Congress, 23, *23*
Founding Fathers, 8
France, 8, 8, 19, *19,* 25
Franklin, Abiah Folger (mother), 9
Franklin, Benjamin, *6, 8, 12, 20, 24, 26, 27*

birth, 9
childhood, 9
death, 27–28, *28*
as delegate to Second Continental Congress, 24, 25
as diplomat, 8, 20–21, *20,* 23, 25
education, 9, 10
eyesight, 16–17
health of, 26, 27
inventions, 9, 16–17
in Pennsylvania Assembly, 17
poetry of, 9–10
as postmaster, 17
as printer, 13, *13,* 14, 14, 15, 28
as printer's apprentice, 9
as Silence Dogood, 11
Franklin, Deborah Read (wife), *12,* 15
Franklin, Francis (son), 15
Franklin, James (brother), 11
Franklin, Josiah (father), 9, 10
Franklin, Sarah (daughter), 15
Franklin stove, 17
Franklin, William (son), 15, 23
French and Indian War, 19, *19,* 20, 21

glass harmonica. See armonica.
Great Britain, 8, 19, 20, 21, 22, 23, 25

Hancock, John, 25

International Swimming Hall of Fame, 9
Intolerable Acts, 22, 23
inventions, 7–8

Jefferson, Thomas, 24
"Join or Die" cartoon, 18, *18*
Junto, 15

kite experiment, 6–7, *6, 16*

Leather Apron Club, 15
Library Company of Philadelphia, 15
lightning rods, 7, *7,* 16
London, England, 20, *20*

New Jersey Colony, 23
New-England Courant newspaper, 11, *11*

odometers, 17

Parliament, 21, 23
Penn, William, 20

The Pennsylvania Gazette newspaper, 15, 18
Pennsylvania Antislavery Society, 27
Pennsylvania Colony, 20
Philadelphia, Pennsylvania, 10, 12–13, *12,* 15
Plan of Union, 18, 19–20
Poor Richard's Almanack, 14, *14,* 15, 28

Quaker religion, 20

Revolutionary War, 8, 23, 25
Riqueti, Honoré-Gabriel, Count of Mirabeau, 28

Second Continental Congress, 24, 25
slavery, 27
The Spectator journal, 10
Stamp Act, 21

Tea Act, 21, 22, 23
Treaty of Alliance, 25, 27
Treaty of Paris, 26, 27

Union Fire Company, 15
University of Pennsylvania, 15

About the Author

ANN HEINRICHS GREW UP IN FORT SMITH, ARKANSAS, AND LIVES IN Chicago. She is the author of more than 100 books on U.S. and world history. After many years as a children's book editor, she enjoyed a successful career as an advertising copywriter. An award-winning martial artist, Ann has traveled extensively throughout the United States, Africa, Asia, and the Middle East.